NO REGRETS

ALL THE THINGS THAT MUST BE SAID,
THE LIFE, LOVE, AND LAUGHTER.

CINDY DILBECK-KUNTZ'S MEMOIR

WRITTEN BY
CAROL ANN EASTMAN

Throughout life, we're given so many opportunities to say what's on our mind, to reveal our true thoughts and feelings. Yet, something always holds us back, forces us to close our mouths and not open up. I can't do that any longer. I refuse to let more time pass without making sure all the words are said, all the feelings are known, and all the hopes are expressed. This is my time. With life, we don't know how much time we have, how much time we're gifted. So in the true spirit of gift-giving; this is my gift to the loves of my life—the loves who have made me the person I am today. Without love, life isn't worth living. And one thing I have learned in the past five years is that life IS worth living, my life is worth living, all because of the loves of my life.

Thank you for taking a chance on me and for reading my love letters. God bless you!

All of my love,
Cindy

CHAPTER
One

"Parenting is the biggest sacrifice one can make, it's putting your life on hold to fulfill the promise of your children's tomorrows." (Frederica Ehimen)

Creeping back through the woods, hiding from everyone, I finally see the opening of brush where the trees clear, and it makes way to the water. Most parents are crazy about their kids following the rules, and mine were, too. But on certain days, my dad bent the rules. And I couldn't be happier about those days. Sneaking through the reservoir to go fishing with my father is one of my most cherished childhood memories. *I search for flowers, knowing my dad is just steps away, hoping for the biggest catch of the year. I feel the comfort of being with Daddy—a feeling of safety and serenity—a feeling only a father can bring.*

You may know them as Walter and Judy Dilbeck, but to me, they're just Mom and Dad. I exist, because those two crazy kids fell in love. And believe me, it was a hard obstacle for them to overcome. Love may have come easy for them, but not for everyone else. It's hard to be in love when you're disliked, right Dad?

My grandfather did not like my dad and refused to accept that my mom loved him. However, my mom was prepared to do anything to spend the rest of her life with him. And she did just that. Running away and eloping was their solution. I probably never thanked you guys for that. So hey, thanks for getting hitched. It is strange how we never think to thank our parents for finding each other and for falling in love. We wouldn't be here if they didn't weather whatever came their way to be together. I'm grateful that they found one another—and that here it is, all these years later, and they've never lost each other.

Like any daughter, I have great memories of my parents. Anyone would call my childhood typical, but to me, it was magical. Looking back on it now, I wouldn't change one thing about it. Dad, I didn't realize until recently how important those days fishing at the Reservoir were to me. Sure, we snuck in, and I never fished. I preferred to sit around and pick flowers while you fussed and messed with the fish. But how many little girls get that time alone with their dads—time that becomes not only etched into their memories, but etched into their hearts forever? Thank you for creating that time with me. I think about those days, and I can still see us there, still feel the warmth of the sunshine, and still feel the carefree moments I felt spending time with my Daddy.

Cancer can come in and keep trying to take so much of me away, but the truth of it is, there is still so much of me that can't be destroyed. And Dad, my past can't be taken from me—those memories with you—those are ours. If there comes a time when I'm not around, (if Dad, always if), just picture me sitting by the Reservoir picking flowers, and we'll both be back there—you and your little girl. That's who I am, Daddy's Little Girl. And you'll always be the strong provider, that man who's always there—for everyone he loves.

They say moms are supposed to be these rule-following, strict people who spend their lives running a household. I am so glad that you didn't get that memo. I was given the mother of all moms. Of course, I got lucky; I got the best of both worlds. Mom, you ran a perfect house—always so caring and loving, to not only Cathy and me, but to Jim and Leroy too. You were the giving and selfless mom to all of us. There were no labels in our house—no stepchildren, stepbrothers, or anything of the sort. We were a family—a family that you nurtured, created, and fostered. Without your lead, we wouldn't have been the family we were.

Looking back at all of our wonderful memories, what makes me laugh the most is that I had the mom who took us girls T.P.ing. Most moms would yell and say, "No way, you can't do that." My mom supplied the toilet paper and the getaway car. And did we really hurt anyone? Not really. After all, that certain someone had it coming; he wasn't exactly Mr. Chivalrous. What we did is create memories—safe memories that we can all still talk about today and laugh our asses off about. I guess since we're on the "No Regrets" kick, I might as well get this over with.

Hey Brad, sorry we T.P.ed your house all the time! Can I get a reprieve or a pardon? I do have brain cancer. Hell yeah, I'm going to play the cancer card. If you had an Ace in BlackJack, you'd use it.

Back to you Mom, I know these past five years have been the worst of your life. I want you to know something; they've been a blessing to me. I got to have you with me through each and every one of them. I couldn't have done this without you. You are the most selfless and caring woman God has ever created. What you've taught me about love and marriage will forever be a part of who I am and who Bella and Evan will be. Your marriage, your dedication to those you love is what I aspire to—what I want my kids to aspire to.

You taught me how to be a mother—how to be caring, loving, kind, giving, and all-forgiving. But you taught me more than that too. You taught me how to fight—how not to put up with bullshit and not get taken advantage of. Mom, if you hadn't taught me how to fight—how to kick and scream to get what I want—then those doctors would've been right five years ago. Because of you, your strength, I learned that nobody goes down without a fight, and Mom, I'm fighting. I am fighting my ass off.

Just a bit ago, we were laughing like we always have. Of course, it was at my expense, but Mom, you taught me to laugh. When life gets so hard, so crazy, just sit back and laugh while you still can. Anyway, I did a little yoga to stretch out my body, to get some circulation moving through my veins. Well one thing is for certain, I absolutely cannot move like I used to. Not even close. I got down. I stretched and worked my body. What I couldn't do was get back up. Mom, you were there—laughing at me—but you were there. You helped me up. If that isn't a metaphor for parenting, then I don't know what is. Every time I fall, you're there to catch me. You're always right there to pick me back up. You're a mom—my perfect mom, through and through.

But I got you back, didn't I? Shortly after, you were snoozing on the couch. And by snoozing, I mean full-out, sound asleep snoring like a freight train. You never would've believed the racket sounding from your lungs. So I did what any modern woman would do to prove a point—I videotaped the ruckus you were creating from deep within you. And God Mom was it funny. Again, laughter has gotten us so far in this tragic battle for survival. Thank you for giving me laughter and always laughing with me—and at me.

Mom and Dad, what I want you to know is that I love you both with all of my heart and all that I am. I appreciate how you've put your lives on hold to help prolong mine. Nothing you have ever done for me has gone unnoticed. My house wouldn't have run as smoothly these past five years if it weren't for you two. Mom, the way you cater to my every whim and need is inspiring. The way you rub my arms and feet is the epitome of a loving and doting mother. The way you both care for Bella when I can't reminds me of how lucky I am—have always been. I had a wonderful childhood. I have no regrets—no complaints. You guys did it all and did it well. I am a lucky little girl with an undying love for her parents. Thank you.

"Like branches on a tree, we grow in different directions, yet our roots remain as one. Each of our lives will always be a special part of the other." (Anonymous)

All great childhoods start with a loving and close-knit family. I couldn't be happier about the family that my parents' marriage fostered for me. I don't know who I'd be or where I would've ended up without my three siblings. Our lives were so interwoven and connected that so much of them is a part of me.

Leroy Dilbeck, I know your life has been a struggle, but I am sincerely proud of you for all the strength you have carried with you over the last thirty years. You're a fighter. Watching your battle with alcohol has paved the path for me, teaching me alternative routes to take in life. I am so saddened by your burden, but inspired by your courage. I pray that someday you find the peace you need to walk away from the vice that holds you hostage. I pray that life grants you the wisdom to know how truly strong and capable you are—because you are. Leroy, you are so strong. Never, ever forget that.

And please Leroy, always know that I have wonderful and fond memories of us—our childhood—memories that I carry with me in my heart. My first picture of you when I close my eyes is always the same. It's you, Leroy, in your preppy and designer clothes, dressing like a million bucks and dazzling everyone with your good looks and charm. I remember how I was the envy of all my friends, because my brother, the model, took me to Beachwood and bought me clothes—clothes that were far pricier than I was used to. My friends were jealous that my brother was so generous and giving—and incredibly good-looking. Because of you, I was the talk of the town, the girl with the hot brother.

Those memories of you—of us—mean so much to me, Leroy. You were and are an integral part of my life.

And Jim, my laughing, loud, hillbilly brother, you taught me so much. You taught me that life is fun and that it is so important to laugh when life gets hard. Believe me, Jim; I've been heeding that advice so much these days. I really don't know what I would've done without it. You taught me to laugh, and I am laughing my way through this illness. I refuse to let it get me down, bring me down; I'm just laughing my pissed-flabby-ass off. (Do you know how hard it is for me to admit that my ass, after all of these years, is now flabby? I have to laugh. Otherwise, I'll cry.)

All of my memories of you involve your giant smile and laughter. There was never a time that I can recall that you weren't having fun—and if there were, they were always few and far between. You are the epitome of the typical older brother, always tickling me, goofing around, and just making my life more fun and more worthwhile. Geez, even recently, you tried to spit your dip (chewing tobacco) out onto the bricks. And what happened? It sprayed all over me. Typical big brother behavior.

Your whimsical and fun demeanor isn't something you ever outgrew. It's who you are, and because of it, even Bella knows that "Uncle Jim Bomb" is the crazy and spirited uncle that she can play and have fun with. And she needs that Jim. She needs you. She needs laughter and joy. She needs to know that life is full of surprises and fun. You can give her that. You're just the uncle to show her how wonderfully exciting life can be. Thank you for being there for her—and for me.

Jim and Leroy, we never grew up with labels. We didn't measure our family in half-siblings or stepchildren or any of that bullshit that so many households do. You are my brothers, full-blooded, full-hearted brothers. And I wouldn't have wanted it any other way. Being your sister has given me the strength and courage to fight many of my battles.

Having two older brothers teaches strength, you both have given me the strength to fight the hardest battle of all. And for that, I am forever grateful. I love you, guys. I never want you to question how much you both mean to me.

No girl should ever have to grow up without the guidance of an older sister. Cathy Daniel, you taught me what a true sisterly bond feels like. Even though you're eight years older than me, (yes I have to remind you), you've always been more like a friend to me than a sister. Of course, we had what others would consider a "typical" sisterly relationship. I stole your clothes and your I.D., and you got mad, but never really cared. That's what sisters do—have done since the beginning of time. I am just so thankful that all the time I've had in this world has gotten to be with you—as your little sister.

I'll never forget when you took Katrina, one of my best friends, and me to see Prince and Pat Benatar. It's moments like those that stick with a person, moments that let you know how truly special you are to someone else. You didn't have to take us. You didn't have to be the sister that put her social life on hold to ensure that I had one for myself. But you did. And I realize now how truly blessed I have been all of these years to have a sister who loves me as much as you do. Maybe you never realized it, but having you as my sister gave me a stronger sense of family and friendship, one that I still carry with me today.

I know that we don't get to see each other all that often, but you should know that the time we do share together, I cherish deeply. I can't believe how incredibly selfless you have been helping me survive this battle. You take care of me—like a loving and protective big sister. How lucky am I?

Our long talks on the phone mean everything to me, because getting to share my thoughts, my dreams, my fears, and my day with my big sister are important to me. And in case I never told you, thank you for

always letting me steal your clothes. I love
you Cathy.

CHAPTER
Three

"I would rather walk with a friend in the dark, than alone in the light." (Helen Keller)

*P*eople think of Pizza Hut and immediately think of the fluffy dough, the mouth-watering breadsticks, and the endless refills of fountain beverages—for dirt cheap. But not me, when I think of Pizza Hut, I think of my lifeline, my best friend, my past, my present, my future—Carrie Morrison. It started as any other part-time waitressing job. We were just two servers who hated their customers, wished they earned better tips, and loathed their closing side-work at the end of each shift. However, Carrie quickly went from my "work friend" to my "best friend."

If you were to drill her, then she'd tell you that it wasn't a love at first sight friendship. She thought I was a bitch. Quite frankly, I was. Have you tried to wait tables at a local pizza joint on a Friday night after a football or basketball game just ended? "Bitch" was probably putting it lightly—and I don't tend to hold my tongue when people are crappy. But after one night of deciding to go out, drink away our server troubles, and dance the night away, Carrie and I foraged a true friendship—a friendship that has withstood the test of time. I'd do anything for her.

Actually, I have done everything (that I could) for her. That's what best friends are for. I am so thankful that I was there for her back in the day when she couldn't conceive. I'm glad that I was able to help by giving her shots to help her get pregnant. God knows, that I have recently needed her more than I have ever needed anyone—and she's always there. At least, I am able to look back on that time and know that I was there for her, because lately, I've leaned on her a hundred times over. To have a best friend who will drop everything for you is a blessing; and Carrie, you are my blessing.

I also want to thank her husband, Tim, for letting her be there for me and for sharing his beautiful wife with me. I don't know what I'd do without both of them. I love that Tim sends me silly and crazy videos—just to make me smile. One of the funniest and craziest things that I love about Carrie is that she does bizarre, eccentric things that makes her so perfectly Carrie, my best friend. I'm going to reveal one of her strange idiosyncrasies. Carrie hides things at Target. Yes, you read that correctly. If she knows she wants something, but isn't going to buy it that day or knows that it is going to go on sale, then she hides it somewhere in the store that nobody else would ever see it. Then, a few days—maybe even weeks—later, she goes back and gets her stash out of her secret hiding place, and buys it. If you're ever at Target and you're looking in the very back corner of a shelf and discover some random object that shouldn't be there, then do what I do, and smile, knowing Carrie Morrison, my best friend, was there.

Carrie, I want you to know how much I love you and value our friendship. It has been the strongest, most important friendship I have ever had. You taught me what true, never-ending, selfless friendship is all about. You've been there for me through it all—showing strength and courage. And I know it hasn't been easy for you to watch your best friend dwindle away like this, but thank you Carrie for never giving up on me. How could I ever give up on myself when I have such a tenacious friend carrying me most of the way?

I ask that no matter what, you keep laughing. Laughter is your weapon. You fight off everything with your laughter. And it is so infectious. When you laugh, everyone laughs with you—or maybe at you. Sometimes, I can't tell. And Carrie, thank you for always being real and honest with me.

Your greatest quality is that you never falter in the truth. You tell it like it is—no matter how hard it is to hear. Thank you for that. You're a true best friend.

CHAPTER
Four

"First love, the love that clings to your heart forever, no matter how much pain it has caused, no matter how many tears have fallen, first love will never leave my soul." (Anonymous)

*F*irst love, it's timeless. Everyone must experience it to truly understand it. Letting go and saying "goodbye" to your first love is always devastatingly and horrifying brutal. But when that goodbye is at his funeral, it is debilitating and forever scarring. It cuts deeper than any pain I've ever experienced.

Roger Golden was my first love—my first everything. It was the kind of first love that everyone should get to have. It was all-consuming, powerful, tumultuous at times, but beyond the realm of anything I ever knew could be possible. I knew I was in love—the kind of love that they wrote about in books, because I never, like ever, wanted to be without him. I could have spent every waking moment with him, and it still wasn't enough to be with him. His goofy personality and genuine smile were everything to me for five full years. He did all the things a first boyfriend should do. He secretly left me roses, took care of me, and was there whenever I needed him. A first love that lasts five years is unthinkable, but I couldn't imagine that love not being every second of those five years.

I also learned that when you truly fall in love with someone, you get his family too. And I was blessed to be a part of the Goldens. His mother and two sisters quickly became part of my family too. To this day, they are still an integral part of my life—still a part of my heart. I love them like the "in-laws that never were."

Roger taught me how to really love someone—how to give my whole heart over to another person and how to hold someone else's heart as my own. When our relationship ended, it was shattering—as all first loves are. But we were young, and our fast-paced, all-encompassing love affair had run its course. We didn't end violently. Never. Nothing with Roger and me could ever have been volatile. We always remained friends, close confidantes. When he went away to college, we both knew that it wasn't meant to be. Even though we tried to hold on, we couldn't. Love that strong—that young—can't last. We grew. We changed. We matured. But we never stopped loving what we had and how we were. He was the start—the beginning of love for me. And I will never regret that or take it lightly.

The day Roger died, a part of me died with him. There is not one single day that goes by that I don't think of him—or that some small reminder whispers in my ear to let me know that he's still there.

'Tis better to have loved and lost than never to have loved at all. (Alfred Lord Tennyson)

*N*o regrets, never a one. That's how I feel. Eric Bauer, you gave me my lifeline, my son, and for that I am forever grateful, forever in your debt. It's funny how you can look back on things and see life so clearly when they were so murky and unclear before. Eric, you are a great, great guy. We just needed to accept that you and aren't compatible. And we did, and I believe you and I are both better off accepting what was obvious to so many others. We don't work, and we couldn't work.

Eric, with you, I learned so much. You taught me patience and compromise. You gave me strength to rebuild and repair. You brought out qualities in me that I had no idea even existed. You helped make the woman I am today—providing me with tenacity and a will to fight—qualities that have only grown and evolved as of recently. Thank you for loving me and for letting me go.

If I hadn't found you and lost you, then Evan wouldn't have Melanie. And Evan needs her—needs a caregiver like her to step up when I can't. Your entire family has been so strong, so kind, and so helpful during all of my struggles and suffering. It eases my pain and fear knowing that the entire Bauer family is there for Evan when he needs you all the most. Thank you for giving me that sense of peace to know that Evan is loved, taken care of, and made a priority. You and your family have shown such grace and character.

Truthfully, I knew that I "was doomed" in the hospital after my first MRI. When you walked into my hospital room with Evan, sobbing, I knew that my prognosis couldn't be good. We never really cried for each other—over each other. To see your tears, your fear, your pain meant that something was gravely wrong. My death sentence was real the moment I saw your face. The worst was coming to fruition—and I could tell it by simply looking into the eyes of my ex-husband.

Maybe we should have cried for each other more—been more open with our emotions. Who knows what could have happened if we had? Eric, I am truly sorry that we didn't work, couldn't make it work, but like I said, I have no regrets. You're happier—more yourself. I'm happier.

Please know that I am grateful to you—for everything.

Everything we had.

Everything we lost.

Everything that is still to come.

"...and she loved a little boy very, very much—even more than she loved herself." (Shel Silverstein)

I held you in my arms, and my very first thought was, "Oh, so this is what love feels like." Evan, I never fully understood or felt the true meaning of love until you were placed in my arms. The second I saw you, held you, smelled you, snuggled you, I knew right then and there that I would die for you—I would give up everything in my entire life just to make you happy.

Evan, you surpassed even my wildest dreams of what a son could be. Growing up, you were the perfect angel. I never understood how people couldn't go places with their babies or their toddlers. I've had so many friends throughout my life who have felt homebound, because their kids couldn't be brought out in public. You were always the flawless child. You never threw temper tantrums, never freaked out, or begged for things at stores. Actually, you caught on quickly. You learned pretty easily that being well behaved and NOT whining for things got you anything you wanted. You were smart and sophisticated as a child, and now, wow, you just amaze me every day.

I also learned pretty quickly that boys are just gross—full out disgusting. I thought it was pretty bad when you pooped outside behind the shed. I remember thinking, "Man, boys can't get any more grotesque than that." But you, always the overachiever at surprising me, decided to prove me wrong. You pooped down the laundry chute. So yes, yes, boys can get even grosser than you ever thought possible.

I also learned fear. When you were five-years-old, your dad and I took you to Disney. We actually won a trip to Disney. It didn't matter that your dad and I were no longer together. We wanted to make you happy, and take you to the "happiest place on earth," and have you experience it with both your mom and dad. Well that trip almost became the most horrific place on earth.

Your dad and I took you on Magic Mountain. Mind you, you were only five at the time. You wanted the front seat. We were the perfectly doting parents, so of course, we allowed you to sit in the front. We strapped you all snugly in, and guess what? You nearly flew right out—like completely out. We had to grab you and pull you back in, bracing you during the rest of the ride.

You were so mad at us. You wouldn't stop crying and you wouldn't talk to us, because we "almost let you die." Now, I can laugh about it, but Evan, it was one of the scariest moments of my life. A life without you isn't a life I ever want to think about—let alone experience. You are the reason FOR my life.

As a mom, you get to raise your son, watch him grow into a strong, powerful man.

However, I never knew it would be so soon. Because of my illness, you had to grow up so fast, so furiously, and I am so very sorry for that. You should have gotten the perfect childhood and flawless adolescence, but this damn cancer had to take all that away from my baby boy. And that just pisses me off. You have no idea. I wanted everything for you. I am sorry that I couldn't give it all to you. But you know what Evan? I got a glimpse of the man you're going to become, and I could not be more proud of you.

Our relationship came full circle not too long ago. But no mater how embarrassing and horrifying it was, it did give me a view of the future, a view of that husband and father you're going to be. And my God, you're going to be perfect. When I fell down the steps and peed myself, I was mortified. But not you. You picked me up like a weightless ragdoll, cleaned me up, and put me back to bed. You didn't bat at an eye at what you had to endure. You just did it— like a man. Evan, I am sorry that our relationship has turned. I'm sorry that you're now taking care of me. I would change that in a heartbeat if I could. I want to care for you, give to you, coddle you. I don't like it this way. I do however love that I got to see the compassionate, loving, gentle man that is growing up right before my eyes.

Now, as your mother, I have things I have to say, things that need to be said. Remember, I am still fighting like Hell to get to say these things each and every day to you until you roll your eyes and cannot take it anymore. But, this is a book of "no regrets," and let's face it; anything can happen in this crazy world. I can walk outside and be struck by lightning tomorrow. Therefore, even though I plan and pray to be here for every milestone in your life, just in case I'm not, I have things to say. That's a mother—always nagging. So just consider this a handheld reminder of my wishes for you and my advice to you. If ever there is a time, you need a "mommy whisper" just refer back to this and remember my hopes and dreams for you.

First and foremost, Evan, please be kind and always help others—be the first one there to help. You've witnessed firsthand how grateful we are as a family to receive help from others. Please, give that same help to someone else in need. Don't wait for them to ask. Offer assistance whenever help is needed—even before it's needed if you can. And if you don't, then quite frankly I'll kick your ass from Heaven. You know I'll find a way to do so, too. I'm feisty; I can get anything done.

When you go to college, don't do drugs. Period. End of story. Nobody in the history of life has ever said, "God, I am so glad I did those drugs." Don't be an idiot and think you're going to love it, and it's going to be a good decision. It is NEVER a good decision. Ever. Yes, I am being a mom here, but hey, that's my job. Get used to it.

Also, college will have all kinds of new and exciting people. Be careful whom you choose to befriend. Don't get into the wrong crowd. They can set you back, pull you down, and destroy your goals. Plus, only the best of the best should get to have Evan Bauer as a friend. Never sell yourself short. It's not fair to you—or me. Look at all the time and energy I've put in to creating such a wonderful young man. Don't you be the one to blow it—especially now—right when you're on the cusp of greatness.

And Evan, please please be good to girls. Be respectful—a perfect gentleman. To treat a woman poorly or disrespectfully is the same as treating me poorly or disrespectfully. We're women; we're strong, confident, and capable, but we're also delicate, fragile, and vulnerable. Always treat us as such.

When you do find the right woman and you're ready to marry her, make sure she is worth it—make sure she deserve you. Evan, always be a loving husband. Listen to her—even when what she's saying might seem mundane and stupid. Sometimes, women just want to talk and be heard. Make sure you're listening, and validate her feelings. That's all we really want—a man to talk to us, acknowledge us, and love us. Be that man. Never give her reason to doubt that you love her. Surprise her—A LOT—give her flowers, special treats, stolen kisses. Make her feel like the only woman in the world. And when she screws up, forgive her. Talk it out.

On the day that you meet your first child, know that the love you're feeling for that baby boy or girl is exactly how I have always felt about you. Remember that feeling and know I am feeling that right now, please never forget it. My love for you is that deep, that true, and that unconditional. When you finally become a "Daddy," be firm, but be gentle. Make sure you tell your kids every single day that you love them—even when they're being little shits. Because let's face it, parenting can be hard, but the reward of fatherhood will greatly outweigh everything else. I promise you that.

Evan, I pray every day that you take care of Bella and that you are always there for her. Please stay together. Love her like I know you can. Be the big brother she needs, because she is going to need you. Watch out for her. She may have a long road ahead of her without a mother, and that is going to be a tough journey for her—for any little girl. Try to make it a bit easier for her. Please son. And try to find the time to continue to foster a relationship with Brandon. You guys can and should find strength in each other. Lean on each other when times get tough.

And finally, never forget that I love you. I am so very proud of you, Evan. You have truly amazed me each and every day of your life. I wish I had 100 more years with you. I'm sorry that I don't. But no matter where I am, or where you are, I will always love you.

CHAPTER
Seven

"True love stories never have endings." (Richard Bach)

It couldn't be more fitting that we met working out when it is exactly what you and I love the most—other than each other, our family, and our faith. It needs to be stated and heard. I wish I could shout it from the rooftops. I stalked Brandon Kuntz until he finally noticed me and asked me out. I'm not shy—have never been shy. When I want something—someone—I get it. Brandon, when you screamed across the room "Want to go to lunch?" it was exactly what I'd been wanting for so long. You have no idea how excited I was. I never knew the 3 Brothers restaurant would be the place that all of my dreams would come true.

During our second date at Bravo, I knew—knew it was forever. There was—is— a connection with you that I have never experienced before. I have loved. I have loved and lost. But you're the first person that made me know what forever love was all about. I never wanted that second date to end. I never want our love story to end, because finally, I have "the real deal." And Brandon, our love story will never end. When you look at Bella, know that our love is transcendent and everlasting. I will love you as long as you are.

I've always wanted to thank you for that trip to the Outerbanks. I loved watching you get closer to Evan and welcome him into your heart and life. Brandon, it means so much to me that you not only love Bella and me, but that you also love Evan as well. You have so much love to give, and I am so lucky that I got to receive all that love—that undying, unconditional love.

Please know that I am truly grateful that I found you and got to have you as my husband. I certainly saved the best for last—without a doubt. Thank you for taking care of me. My God, you never complain, never grumble. You are selfless and giving and such a wonderful man. It breaks my heart that I cannot grow old with you, but it certainly warms my heart that I was even blessed with you at all. How did I get so lucky to find you?

I know that through all of this, you have kept so much hidden, so much inside to stay strong for me. I am sorry that I had to burden you with the pain, the worry, and the fear. But thank you for being the strong, giving man that you are. Thank you for being my husband, my true love story. Marrying you on Sweetest Day was undoubtedly the sweetest day of my life. I married the sweetest man I've ever encountered on a day meant for us.

And the future? I'm sorry that I cannot guarantee you a million tomorrows. But I can guarantee you that I will love you for every tomorrow that comes. Brandon, you have such a loving and supportive family. There is going to come a time when you are going to need them—really need to lean on them—please do so. Let them hold you, carry you, and support you through the pain. Don't try to shoulder it all. You've carried enough pain—enough worry. When it comes time for you to crumble, allow yourself that. You owe it to yourself—to us. Grieve for us; I know I do. You can too.

And when the time comes, fall in love again. You have so much love to give. Don't hold it in—give it to someone else—someone who deserves it. But my God, do not marry a hoe. I'm serious. You're pretty shy. Don't let some skank snatch you up and take advantage of you. Find someone who actually deserves a perfect and wonderful husband like you. Please make sure she really loves Bella and treats her well. I pray that she has a strong Christian faith, so you both can grow together in God's love. Let her be someone my little girl can look up to and learn from. You have my blessing to love again. Actually, I am making it mandatory that you do fall in love again. Don't spend your days alone. You don't deserve that, and I don't want that for you.

When you do fall in love, please still remember me and take time to talk about me. Tell Bella stories about me. Let her know how fun I once was and how much I loved to laugh and make other people laugh. Laughter is so important. Make sure she knows that. I want my stories to be told with laughter and fun—please tell them that way.

I do have one more thing to say. I was wrong. It isn't "until death do us part." Brandon Kuntz, my love for you far exceeds that. Always.

CHAPTER
Eight

"And I realized when you look at your mother, you are looking at the purest love you will ever know." (Mitch Albom)

I have always said that you, Bella, are my princess. However, I certainly didn't want to be so "Disney" literal in the sense of that word. All those Disney princesses grow up without a mother. But now that I think about it, they all do grow up to be strong, smart, independent, beautiful women who do the right thing. So yes, Bella, you are and always will be my princess—my beautiful, smart, strong, independent princess.

I have to thank you for the past five years. You have been the single guiding force as to why I am still here, still fighting. I couldn't give up and throw in the towel, not when I had you to love, to teach, to hug, and to be there for. Oh Bella, I so wanted to be there for every single milestone in your life. I am so sorry I have been sick for all of your life. I am so sad that you didn't get to see and really witness whom your mom is. I used to be so fun, so full of life. Nobody could keep me down or stop me. I was always on the go. I hate that you never got to see that part of me. I swear, if I could, I would show you how crazy and fun I am. I would show you true laughter and a true zest for life. I pray that the stories that come back about me make you laugh and make you want to DO. Do everything, Bella. Experience all that life has to offer.

I want you to know that when I found out that I was having a little girl, it was the greatest moment of my life. I wanted a girl so badly. I couldn't wait to have that unbreakable mother-daughter bond. Now, just hearing your sweet voice can bring me to tears. I am just so filled with love. I love hearing you talk and hearing you laugh. Your voice keeps me going. It takes the darkness and fear out of my days, bringing me more light than you could ever realize.

There are so many things that I want to say to you, so many things that I want to teach you. It shatters me that I may not be the one who gets to teach you and guide you. In case I don't, I want you to have this little reminder of what your mom wants for you, what she prays you'll have and do. Think of this as your constant reminder that I am always here for you and with you—even if I'm not.

Bella, honey, I want you to make friends---many many friends. But it is more important for YOU to be a good friend to others. Be nice to girls—even when girls aren't very nice. I have to be honest with you; girls are mean. Don't fall into that cycle. Don't let others treat you poorly and please please don't treat other badly. Be strong and always stand up for yourself, but be gentle and kind. Friends are so important; they get you through the hardest, darkest times of your life. They'll be there for you—if you are a good and worthy friend to them.

And boys? Oh boy! Daddy is going to just love when boys start coming around. Your best bet is to just stay away from them. I'm just kidding, honey. You'll fall in love. You'll get your heartbroken. And you'll fall in love again. And Bella, it will all be worth it. But in the beginning, when you're young, naïve, and impressionable, just be friends with boys. There's no rush to "mess around" with them. You don't need that. And for the love of God, don't dress like a hooker! There's going to come a time when you THINK that showing off your "goods" is a good idea. It never is. Never. Leave things to the imagination—don't flaunt anything. You're better than that. You're always better than what everyone else is doing. Remember that. I made my fair share of mistakes when I was growing up, so I know how you can "follow the leader" right down the wrong path. Try to be smarter than that. Try to BE the leader and lead the right way.

I want you to always know that I love you—more than you will ever imagine. I owe you the last five years of my life. Without you, I wouldn't have fought as long and as hard as I have. You have no idea how crushing it was to finally get my wish and then to hear that I might not be around to actually enjoy my dream come true. You really are my dream come true. I am so proud of you. I will always be proud of you. You are so smart and so incredibly funny. Promise me that you'll never lose your wit and sense of humor. Always keep having fun. Make sure your life is full of laughter and fun; and every time you laugh, like a good, strong belly laugh, think of me. Carrie and Uncle Jim will always find a way to make sure you have that laughter. They're good for that—cling to them when you need it.

Bella, I have some crazy advice for you, Mommy's words of wisdom:

*When you start your period, use pads first. Don't be embarrassed. Your dad understands. Just walk right up to him and say, "Dad, I need pads. I started my period." Trust when I say that your dad has seen his fair share of medical things, and he never falters in his undying love and never passes judgment. He's a good one to have around. Starting your period is a rite of passage—nothing to be scared of or humiliated about. Be proud to be a woman. I am so proud to be a woman. Go ahead and take your time before using a tampon. They hurt. And don't read the box on "how to" insert them. Nobody stands with her foot on the toilet to get it in. Nobody. Just talk to your friends; they'll tell you the truth.

*When you start wearing make up, just remember that a little goes a long way. You don't need to cake it on your face and look like a clown. You and your dad are probably going to fight over when you can start wearing it. I would say some lip gloss when you're 13-years-old and some blush and mascara when you're 14-years-old. Save the rest for high school. But you know what?

You're beautiful just the way you are. You don't need makeup.

*And again, don't dress like a hooker. I can't emphasize this enough. You will attract all the wrong boys—the boys that go after "that," aren't the types of boys you want. Trust me.

*You can style your hair any way you want. Just don't make it blue or purple. You have such gorgeous hair; you don't want to ruin it by making it look unnatural. You really are my natural beauty.

*Sex. Don't have it. Wait until you're married. Maybe not even then. I'm just teasing. Fall in love. Get married. And then experience everything you want with your husband. You will be so glad you waited—and so will he.

*Please do well in school. Take your time and make every grade count. I want you to go to college and find your own way in life. Don't rely on someone to take care of you and pay your bills. Be strong. Be independent. But when you do fall in love, fall hard and fall forever. Don't build walls around yourself. Let a loving, strong, deserving Christian man in.

*And be fearless. Conquer life. Never let anything scare you from experiencing it— unless it's "dumb," like drugs or careless, reckless behavior. Don't do anything because others say it's "cool." Make your own decisions. Embrace your life—be happy and proud to live your life. Have a life that makes you happy and fulfilled.

Oh Bella, please know that I wish more than anything I could be with you for all of this. Just know that no matter what you do, where you are, I am always with you. I love more than you will ever truly understand. But one day, when you have a beautiful little girl of your own, you'll get it. You will understand how much your little voice fills my heart with more love than I ever knew was possible. You are my princess.

"I have been crucified with Christ. It is no longer I who live, but Christ who lives in me. And the life I now live in the flesh I live by faith in the Son of the God, who loved me and gave himself for me." Galatians 2:20

*I*t should be no surprise to those who really know me that one of my "love letters" goes to God. I love Him with all that I am. I never questioned Him or doubted Him. My faith in Him and his plan never faltered through all of his. Of course, I struggled with "Why me?" and at times, I got angry, but I never doubted that He was with me, guiding me and loving me all the way. I kept reminding myself that there were people who are far worse off than I am. I know that there are starving people in the world, people who can't walk or talk, people who have nobody, and I realized that even though I was fighting the hardest battle of my life, I was blessed with the life, family, and love that I have been given.

This awful, horrifying cancer took so much from me, but I followed God's way and embraced everything it gave me too. It showed me how many people are so selfless and giving and would do anything for my family and me. I had no idea how loved and cared about we were until faced with this disease.

For instance, I gained a whole new family and close-knit group of friends at Powerhouse Gym. The people there not only opened their arms and their gym to me, but they opened their hearts to me too, giving me more love and support than I could imagine. That was God's way of leading me to peace and to strength, showing me that love can be found anywhere at any time.

I have gained stronger relationships and more meaningful connections. My high school friends and I became closer than we were as giggly teenagers, and I am thankful for their undying and everlasting love and support. Friendships like that withstand the test of time and adolescent drama. God's love taught me that.

Through all of this, I learned that I can be the strength that others need—even when I feel weaker than I have ever been in my life. For the first time, I got to be other people's inspiration. People looked up to me, aspired to be as strong and as determined as I am. Strangers called me, looking for my advice, asking for my guidance on how to fight when the fight was diminishing within them.

In the beginning, right after my terminal diagnosis, I was struggling. I admit that. I was angry. I felt doomed and betrayed. I wanted a life—a long life with everyone I love. I had a six-week old baby to care for, nurture, and spend the rest of my life loving. How could I have only three months to live? It wasn't fair. I was pissed—and rightfully so, I thought.

But then, He changed all that anger for me. I was supposed to be getting all of my affairs in order, because my death sentence had been set. I had three months to live. My family did exactly what they would do in such a situation. We had a party, of course. All of my friends and family were going to shower me with love and affection before I went do Duke for treatments and tests. Therefore, I needed to get ready and make myself look fabulous for the event. As I was blow-drying my hair, I heard a whisper. I turned the dryer off, and there it was again. "I am with you, my child." It was crystal clear, spoken in the breeze and right into my ear. Nobody was around.

God was speaking to me.

And with that one deeply profound statement, all my fear, anger, and worry vanished. I was his child, and He was going to take care of me every step of the way. When I was weak, He would carry me. That was the deal; that was the plan. Just as I would do anything for Evan and Bella, my children, God was going to do everything for me, his child. It was an epiphany that I cannot explain, but that will stay with me forever. He gave me the peace and reassurance that I was seeking. And for that, and for everything else, I will always love Him.

CHAPTER
Ten

"Find the love you seek, by first finding the love within yourself. Learn to rest in that place within you that is your true home." (Sri Sri Ravi Shankar)

I will admit the truth. I never loved my own life and myself until it was put on the line and threat of losing it became a reality. But now, I see the truth, the big picture. Life a precious, precious gift—one that should never be taken for granted or devalued. It is the most valuable gift we are given. We need to cherish our lives as much as humanly possible.

In all honesty, as much as it saddens me to admit this, I didn't know how important life is, especially as an adolescent. God, I hate admitting this to Evan or to Bella, but as a teenager, I got down, really down. It breaks my heart that one time, I thought life was so disposable that I actually tried to take my own life. Can you imagine me, Cindy Kuntz, giving up and trying to end her life like that? I can't even remember being that lost and that depressed, but I was. I was wrong—so wrong.

There is NEVER a reason to give up—never. Life is too beautiful. Life is worth fighting like Hell for. I thank God every day that my rash attempt at suicide failed. Look at all I have been gifted: my children, my husband, my family, and a world of friends that would drop everything to care for me and for my family. What a beautiful and priceless gift life is. How could I ever have even toyed with the idea of throwing it all away? Nothing, not one thing, is more precious and important than this one life we have been given to live. I hope both Evan and Bella know how precious every single second their lives are and that they do not take one of those moments for granted and waste it away. Life, the darkest parts and the brightest parts, are worth every minute.

When I would get down and helpless during this battle and the guilt would overtake me, I would remember how I have been living on borrowed time. The time that I have been given has meant everything to me. I have learned to cherish every moment life has to offer. Life isn't about giving up. Life is about living. I hope that I taught my children how to fight—fight for the life they want. I am so glad that I learned to love myself and love my life, because it has made all the difference these past few years. When you love your life and love yourself, loving everything else comes so easily and so purely. I now welcome love—from anyone and anything.

I have no regrets. Everything that I ever needed to say has been said. Everything that I ever needed to feel has been felt. I have felt love beyond my wildest dreams and I have given all of my love to those who have meant the most to me. I am grateful that I had the opportunity to learn so much about myself. I wasted no time and left nothing unsaid. I am going to continue to fight for the life I love and love with all of my heart and soul. Because in the end, love is all that matters.

Thank you for sharing my life and being a part of my "No Regrets Love Story." Each and every one of you has touched my life and made my life worth fighting for. I love you all and will always love you. I am blessed that each of you has touched an important part of my heart and soul. I will be forever grateful.

AUTHOR'S Note

It is important to know that Cindy and I were not high school "besties" or anything like that. We didn't grow up at each other's houses, braiding each other's hair, or telling secrets into the wee hours of the night. In all honesty, Cindy and I weren't friends growing up. We were friendly. Cindy and I both attended Green High School in Akron, Ohio; she graduated two years before I did. Basically, our friends were friends. I mainly knew her, because she was "my friend's brother's girlfriend." That's how close we were.

However, when Facebook came along, our friendship circle tightened. Social media has a way of bringing people together. I started seeing Cindy's posts about her brain cancer, and I watched from afar as her pictures revealed a battle that was excruciating and terrifying. I knew she had just had a baby girl and her prognosis was not favorable. I began stalking her posts and pictures, destroyed by the fact that she may die when she had an infant at home. As a motherless daughter, the reality kept me up at night. I hated that her baby girl may possibly grow up without a daughter. It broke my heart for Cindy and for Bella.

I had a fleeting thought, "I should write a book for her, so Bella can know more about her mother." The thought was fleeting, because how was I supposed to write a book about someone I didn't really know myself. The idea was absurd—not to mention invasive. What was I going to do? Call her up and say, "Hey, I'm going to write a book about you." That's just weird.

After seeing more and more posts, I started becoming inspired by Cindy. She was working out and helping others, all while battling a death sentence. Who does that? She was facing every mother's worst fear, and yet, she was fighting like crazy to change the prognosis. She is a warrior, a fighter, and I was increasingly motivated by her.

Finally, I made the call and asked her to dinner. She immediately and readily accepted. To this day, I cannot imagine what was going through her head when I called her out of the blue like that. She must've thought I was a whack-a-doodle. We went to dinner, and she talked like we were old friends. We shared stories and horrors. We even cried together that night. I told her stories about how I felt when my mom died; she told me how she felt about leaving her children. We were immediately connected. By the end of the night, I told her the real reason why I'd wanted to meet with her. She loved the idea and was incredibly touched by my offer.

Cindy and I only met a few times for interviews and questions. I am so grateful to have had those meetings. Of course, I got to learn about Cindy and all the important people in her life, while also being taken on a journey of her battle with brain cancer. But more than that, I got to learn about myself.

With each story she told, I was forced to look at my own life, my own mortality, and I realize that I need to live my life more like Cindy lives hers. I need to be more open and loving. I need to be more giving and selfless. Cindy leads a life that others should emulate and aspire to. She loves wholly and entirely. After only two visits there, Cindy hugged me, kissed me, and told me she loved me. And you know what? I felt it. I felt her love. She gives it freely. I love her. I love her for all that she taught me and showed me. Everyone should get the opportunity to have a Cindy in his or life, because the world is a brighter place. I didn't get decades with her friendship and love. I got less than a year, but I will tell you, that year was worth it. It was worth it, because she changed me. I am thankful that Cindy has touched my life, and I will be forever grateful.

I definitely use the term, "book," lightly when referring to this document. I know many readers expect more than 66 pages when they read a book. However, Cindy wanted to say what she needed, and I respect her for getting her words and feelings out. Everything has been said. It is important to me that her family and friends read what has been in her heart these past five years. They deserve to know. She deserves to reveal it all.

All proceeds from this "Love Letter" will go directly to the Kuntz family. For every $2.99 download of this document, $2.09 will go to them. Everyone knows how financially draining a five-year battle with cancer can be. The medical bills alone are astronomical. I wanted to start a "Go Fund Me" account and attach it to the document. However, not all of the funds would go directly to the Kuntz family then. I don't want them to worry about their bills. It's not right. Therefore, I am going to give you the opportunity to donate funds directly to Brandon Kuntz's Paypal account. Here is the email account that is linked to his Paypal: kuntzwayne@yahoo.com

If you have your own Paypal account, donating is simple. All you have to do to is go to your Paypal account, and click on "Send Money to Family and Friends." Then, input Brandon's email and the amount, you'd like to send. And Voila! He will receive the money. Nobody should have to worry about money when there are so many other important things to worry about. Every little bit helps. Even just downloading this document and allowing the family to receive $2.09 is helpful. I just want the family to focus on Cindy and each other—not worry about money. It is the least I can do.

Thank you so much for your time, your love for Cindy, and for all that you have done to make Cindy's life wonderful.

Always,
Carol Ann Eastman
Forever touched by Cindy, a wonderful friend and warrior.

Made in the USA
Lexington, KY
16 January 2017